WILD WATER

Wakeboarding

BY S.L. HAMILTON

A&D Xtreme
An imprint of Abdo Publishing | www.abdopublishing.com

Visit us at
www.abdopublishing.com

Published by Abdo Publishing Company, a division of ABDO, PO Box 398166, Minneapolis, Minnesota 55439. Copyright ©2016 by Abdo Consulting Group, Inc. International copyrights reserved in all countries. No part of this book may be reproduced in any form without written permission from the publisher. A&D Xtreme™ is a trademark and logo of Abdo Publishing Company.

Printed in the United States of America, North Mankato, Minnesota.
062015
092015

 PRINTED ON RECYCLED PAPER

Editor: John Hamilton
Graphic Design: Sue Hamilton
Cover Design: Sue Hamilton
Cover Photo: Glow Images
Interior Photos: AP-pgs 4-5, 10-11, 20, 22-23, 24-25, 26 & 27; Corbis-pgs 7, 8-9 & 13; Glow Images-pgs 1, 16-17, 21 & 32; iStock-pgs 2-3, 9 (inset), 12 (both images), 13 (inset), 14-15, 18-19, 28-29 & 30-31; Library of Congress-pg 6.

Websites
To learn more about Wild Water action, visit booklinks.abdopublishing.com. These links are routinely monitored and updated to provide the most current information available.

Library of Congress Control Number: 2015930953

Cataloging-in-Publication Data

Hamilton, S.L.
  Wakeboarding / S.L. Hamilton.
   p. cm. -- (Wild water)
  ISBN 978-1-62403-753-5
  1. Wakeboarding--Juvenile literature.   I. Title.
  797.3--dc23

2015930953

Contents

Wakeboarding

Wakeboarding is a fast-paced, trick-driven extreme water sport. It combines waterskiing, surfing, skateboarding, and snowboarding. A rider holds onto a tow rope and is pulled by a boat, personal watercraft (PWC), or cable. The wake that is created allows the rider to perform cuts, carves, rotations, jumps, and spins. More fun comes by getting big air!

XTREME DEFINITION – Brake the ache: The first ride of the season.

History

In the early 1900s, people rode boards called aquaplanes, which were towed behind motorboats. This was one of the first types of wakeboarding. However, modern surfing and waterskiing were the foundations for today's sport of wakeboarding.

A man aquaplaning in about 1920.

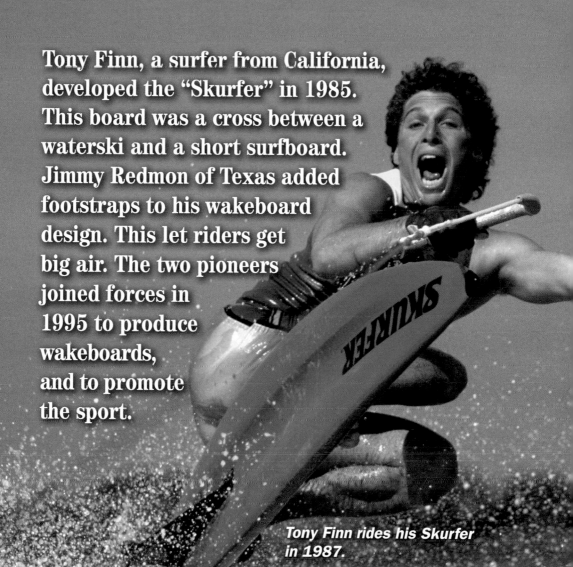

Tony Finn, a surfer from California, developed the "Skurfer" in 1985. This board was a cross between a waterski and a short surfboard. Jimmy Redmon of Texas added footstraps to his wakeboard design. This let riders get big air. The two pioneers joined forces in 1995 to produce wakeboards, and to promote the sport.

Tony Finn rides his Skurfer in 1987.

XTREME FACT – Jimmy Redmon founded the World Wakeboarding Association (WWA) in 1989. The WWA today supervises wakeboarding rules and competitions.

Parts of a Wakeboard

Tail (back)

W akeboards look a lot like snowboards. However, they are shorter in length and slightly wider.

Straps (secures feet in boots)

Rails or Edges (sides)

Bindings/Boots

Nose (front)

Several factors go into choosing a wakeboard. The size of the rider determines the length of the wakeboard needed. Heavier riders need longer wakeboards. Riders being pulled by a cable at a wakeboarding cable park need a different board than those being pulled by a boat or a personal watercraft (PWC).

Fins (ridges on the bottom of the wakeboard that help the rider turn)

Rope →

← Handle

XTREME FACT – A young wakeboarder just learning to ride is called a "grom," or "grommet."

Safety Equipment

A rider who hits water at a fast speed can be knocked unconscious. Many people wear wakeboard helmets to protect their heads. They also wear wakeboard vests designed with large armholes for ease of movement. The vests are personal flotation devices (PFDs) and provide impact protection.

Wakeboarders must check their rope each time they go out. Wakeboard rope has nearly no stretch. It is lightweight but very strong, with a tensile strength of at least 2,000 to 4,000 pounds (907 to 1,814 kg). It is designed to stand up to sun, salt, and abrasion. However, even strong rope may break. No one wants to be whipped by a snapped rope.

Stance

Similar to snowboarding, wakeboarding offers riders a choice of stances. A rider can go right-foot forward ("goofy foot") or left-foot forward ("regular foot").

Goofy Foot: Right-Foot Forward

Regular Foot: Left Foot Forward

XTREME FACT – To tell which foot should go forward, a person can be unexpectedly gently pushed from behind. Whichever foot goes forward first is the forward foot. Other ways to find the forward foot is to note which foot goes in first when putting on a pair of pants or which foot is used to kick a ball.

Beginners often stand with the rear binding fairly far back on the board. This is the most stable position. It helps riders learn deepwater starts, as well as beginning hops, jumps, and tricks. Experienced riders move their bindings more toward the center of the wakeboard. A centered stance allows for advanced tricks such as spins and riding backwards.

Speed

Getting up on the board is the first challenge of wakeboarding. Unlike waterskiing, the boat or personal watercraft (PWC) driver needs to pull the rider up *slowly*. A rider who is pulled up too fast will end up painfully face-planting into the water. Once up, first-time riders are towed at a slow rate of 12 to 14 miles per hour (19 to 23 kph).

XTREME QUOTE – *"If the rider is screaming at you to slow down, listen to them."* –Greg Young, Wakeboarding Instructor, Northwest Riders

Experienced riders are pulled at speeds of around 25 miles per hour (40 kph). These fast speeds create a cleaner and firmer wake. This makes it easier to perform complicated tricks, or achieve big air. It is also more dangerous. It is important for the rider to communicate to the driver about what speed is comfortable.

Rope Length

One important part of wakeboarding is how long the rider's rope should be. Wakeboarders want to ride in the area where it's clean and solid, just behind the white mushy spray. If a rider goes into the lip (where the wake is cresting over itself), it's a recipe for a fall.

XTREME FACT – *Instructors often shorten the wakeboard rope to help beginners learn to clear the wake.*

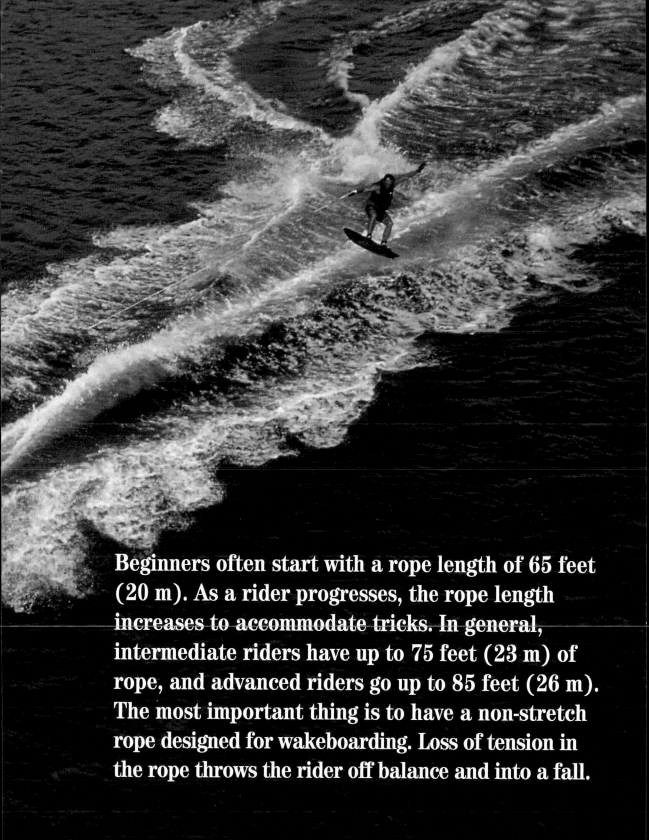

Beginners often start with a rope length of 65 feet (20 m). As a rider progresses, the rope length increases to accommodate tricks. In general, intermediate riders have up to 75 feet (23 m) of rope, and advanced riders go up to 85 feet (26 m). The most important thing is to have a non-stretch rope designed for wakeboarding. Loss of tension in the rope throws the rider off balance and into a fall.

Surface Tricks

Tricks performed while a rider is on the water are called surface tricks. These include such colorful names as the butterslide, body slide, bunny hop, no hander, surface 180 and 360.

A wakeboarder performs a surface trick.

XTREME FACT – Wakeboard athletes need a strong grip, good knee and ankle strength, as well as muscles in their forearms, core (abdomen), back, thighs, and neck.

Grabs & Spins

Grabs are tricks in which a rider grasps the wakeboard while in midair. Many of these tricks look like those performed with skateboards or snowboards. Tricks may be as straightforward as nose or tail grabs. There are also many colorful names, such as Canadian bacon, roast beef, and chicken salad.

A wakeboarder performs a nose grab.

Spins are when a rider and board rotate in the air. Many spins are named after the degree of spin achieved, such as 180, 360, 540, 720, 900, and even 1080. Spins such as baller and osmosis involve passing the handle between the legs and from one hand to another. Flatline spin and wrapped are tricks in which there is no handle pass in the spin.

A wakeboarder performs a 360 trick.

XTREME FACT – Parks Bonifay landed the first wakeboarding 1080 spin in 1999.

Inverts or Flips

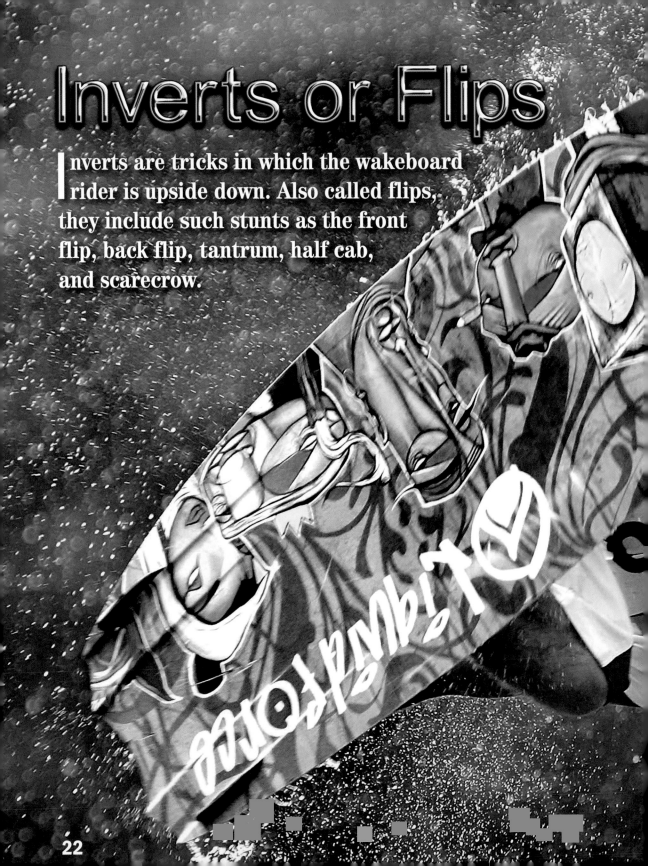

Inverts are tricks in which the wakeboard rider is upside down. Also called flips, they include such stunts as the front flip, back flip, tantrum, half cab, and scarecrow.

Handle-pass inverts
involve a rider not only
going upside down, but
also performing a spin
in which the handle is
passed while in the air.
Some colorful names
include the dum dum,
fruit loop, Pete Rose,
Moby Dick, tootsie roll,
and fat chance.

Raley-Based Tricks

Raley-based tricks are often some of the first air tricks learned. These tricks are nicknamed "Superman" because of the rider's position.

In raley-based tricks, the wakeboard is slightly above the rider's head, with the rider's body fully extended. The rider does not invert or flip. The air raley has the rider's body in a Superman-flying position. Other raley-based tricks include the hoochie glide, the batwing, and the square raley.

Competitions

There are many local, national, and international wakeboarding competitions. The Pro Wakeboard Tour and King of Wake are both organized by the World Wakeboarding Association.

Keenan Allen competes in the 2014 Pro Wakeboard Tour in Grand Rapids, Michigan.

The International Waterski & Wakeboard Federation organizes the Pan American Wakeboard Championship and Wakeboard World Cup. These are held in international locations, such as Argentina, Australia, Brazil, Canada, China, Italy, and the Netherlands.

Marcelo Girardi competes in the 2007 Pan American Wakeboard Championship in Rio de Janeiro, Brazil.

XTREME FACT – Cable wakeboarding will be a trial sport at the 2016 Olympic Games in Rio de Janeiro, Brazil.

Dangers

An important part of wakeboarding is learning how to fall. Riders often "catch an edge." This means that one side of the board has gone underwater. This makes the board stop, but not the rider. The rider is propelled forward, usually hitting the water hard with the front or back of the head. The rider can be knocked unconscious.

Maintaining a safe boat speed for the rider's skill level is important. It's also good to have two people in the boat. This allows the driver to do nothing but drive, while a spotter watches the rider.

XTREME FACT – Bail, eye-opener, face-plant, wreck, and wipeout are all wakeboarding terms for falling.

Glossary

BIG AIR
A high jump in such sports as wakeboarding, snowboarding, and skateboarding. The rider gets airborne, leaving the water, snow, or ground to fly through the air.

CABLE PARK
A place where wakeboarders are pulled by an electronically run cable, instead of a boat or PWC. The wakeboarder can perform tricks or move up and across a series of obstacles. (A cable park is shown on this page.)

PERSONAL FLOTATION DEVICE (PFD)
Also known as a life jacket. A life-saving device designed to keep a person afloat even if he or she has been knocked out. Different styles are available to allow needed freedom of movement for boaters, canoers, kayakers, and PWC riders.

PERSONAL WATERCRAFT (PWC)

A water vehicle mainly designed for individual use. PWCs are used for play, transportation, and racing. They are often known by the manufacturers's names: Jet Ski, Sea-Doo, and WaveRunner.

SPIN

A trick where the rider makes a half turn (180 degrees), full turn (360 degrees), or multiple turns. This can include surface turns or, more commonly, spins in the air.

TENSILE STRENGTH

The force required to pull something, such as a rope or cable, to the point where it breaks. Wakeboarding rope has a very strong tensile strength. It would take 2,000 to 4,000 pounds (907 to 1,814 kg) of force to break a new wakeboarding rope.

UNCONSCIOUS

A person who is not awake or aware of what is going on around them.

WORLD WAKEBOARDING ASSOCIATION (WWA)

A governing body that supervises wakeboarding rules, tricks, events, contests, and competitor rankings.

Index